Colour Land 3

Pupil´s Book

AF865374

Anja Auerswald
Ines Barth
René Marth

Berater
Solveig Haegeler
Silke Weinert

Ernst Klett Verlag
Stuttgart • Leipzig

Erklärung der Symbole

4 Activity Book-CD mit Angabe der Tracknummer

1.13 Teacher's Book-CD mit Angabe der Tracknummer

Inhaltsverzeichnis

Welcome to the British Isles

1 Point at the right picture.

Scotland

Loch Ness

England

Buckingham Palace

Here lives the Queen.

Wales

There are many castles in Wales.

Northern Ireland

You can see a lot of sheep in Northern Ireland.

Landeskunde

Let’s speak English!

Diese englischen Wörter kenne ich schon.

1 Point and say.

Me and my family

1.06

1.07

1. Listen to the story.

2. Who is Lily?

3. Who is Ben?

4. Who is John?

5. What are the children wearing?

* How is Nelly?

Numbers, colours, family

1.08
2

1 One, two, three. Sing the song.

1.10

2 Tony's family. Listen and point.

1.11
3

3 Red and yellow. Sing the song.

Red and yellow and blue and green, blue and green, blue and green.

Red and yellow and blue and green and white and pink and brown.

Übungsseite

Feelings

1 Feelings. Look and say.

Nelly is ...

Nelly is ...

Nelly is ...

2 If you're happy. Listen and do.

1.13

4

If you're  and you know it, clap your hands.

If you're  and you know it, stamp your feet.

If you're  and you know it, say boo-hoo.

3 Sing the song.

1.14

4 Read the text. Then make your own text.

My name is Lizzy.
What's your name?

Dialoge führen, Differenzierung

Let's go to school

1.19

1. Listen to the story.
2. How many children can you see?
3. What colour is Ben's school bag?
4. What can Ben not find?

5. What has Nelly got in her pencil-case?

* What else is on the tables?

School things

1.20

1 What have they got? Listen and point.

Don’ts

1.21

6

2 Do the chant.

Don’t put  on your teacher’s desk.

Don’t put  on your teacher’s desk.

Don’t put  on your teacher’s desk.

Don’t put 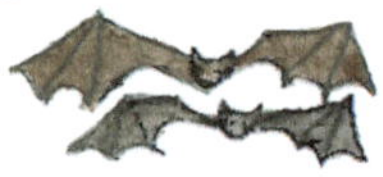 on your teacher’s desk.

Don’t put  on your teacher’s desk.

Don’t put  on your teacher’s desk.

My pencil case

1 Point and ask your partner.

What is it?

It's a ...

2 What is in your pencil case? Talk to your partner.

3 Read the text. Then make your own text.

Good morning.
I'm Claire from London.
I have got a pink school bag.
What colour is your school bag?

My body and my clothes

1.27

1. Listen to the story.
2. Who can you see in the picture?
3. What is Lily wearing?
4. What is Ben wearing?

5. How many T-shirts can you see?

***** What is Nelly wearing?

6. How many umbrellas can you see?

Body and clothes

1.28

8

1 Head, shoulders ... Sing the song.

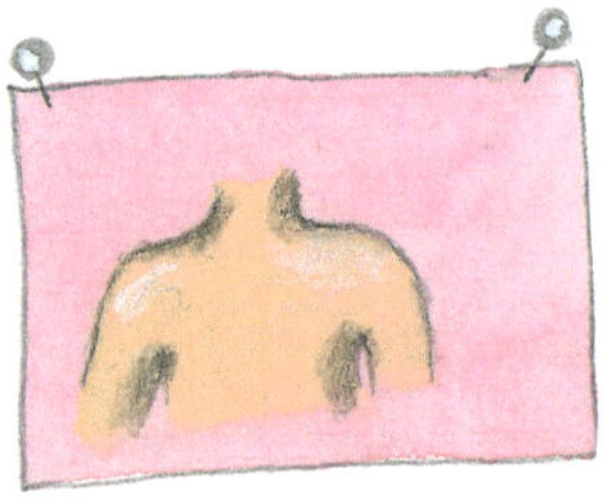
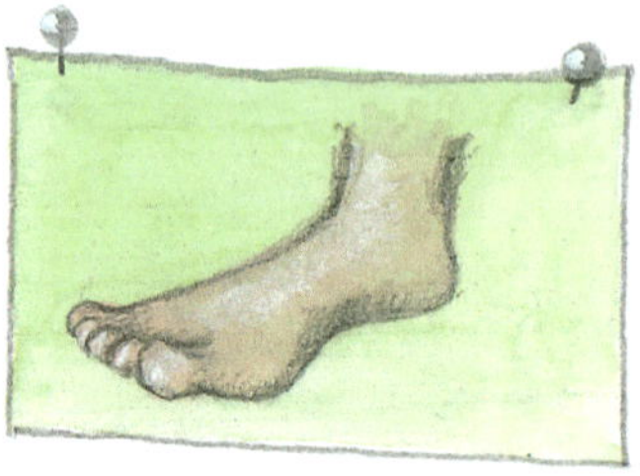

Head, shoulders, knees and toes, knees and toes.

Head, shoulders, knees and toes, knees and toes.

Eyes and ears and mouth and nose.

Head, shoulders, knees and toes, knees and toes.

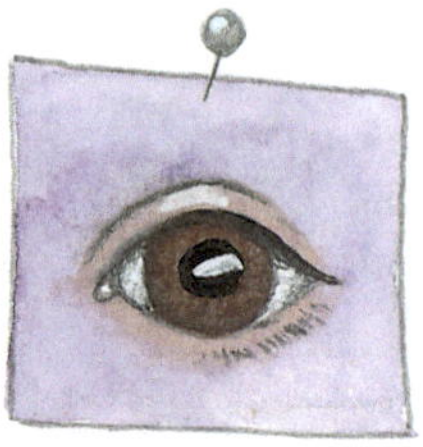

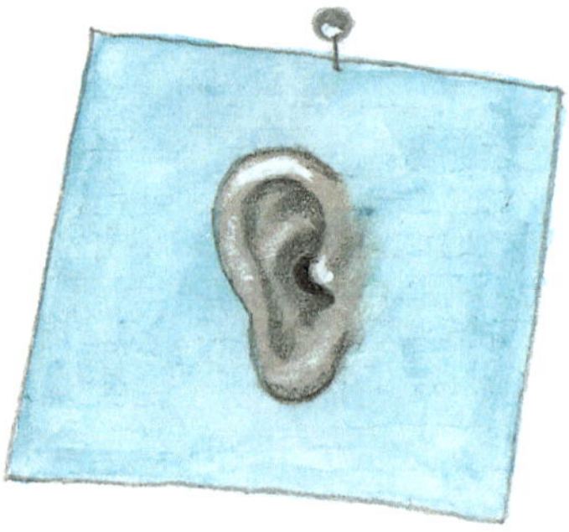
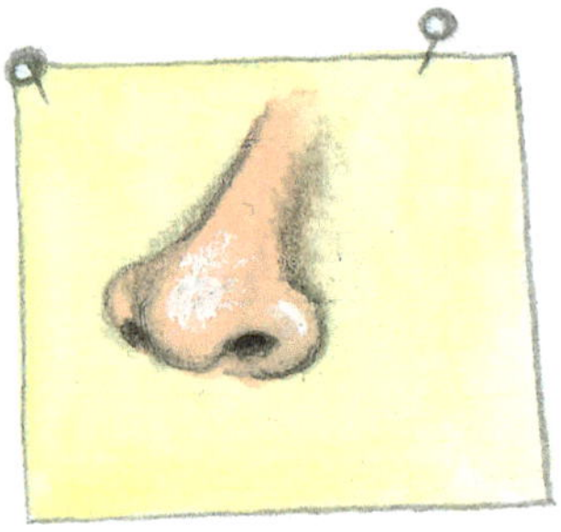

2 School uniforms. What have they got? Look and say.

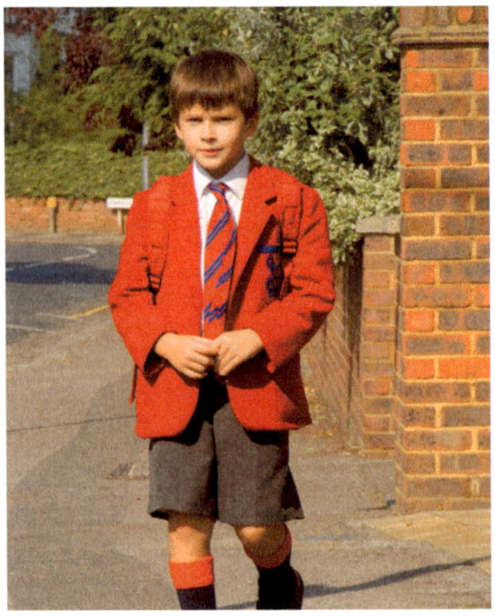

The boy has got ...

The girl has got ...

Clothes

1 Ask your partner.

2 Read the text. Then make your own text.

Hi.
I'm Mark.
I live in Florida.
I like shorts. And you?

Let's play!

1.35

1. Listen to the story.
2. Who can you see in the picture?
3. What is Lily doing?
4. What is Ben doing?

5. How many stockings can you see?

6. How many stars can you see?

7. Can you see an angel?

* Are the presents for Ben?

Toys and hobbies

1 Count the toys. How many toys can you see?

I can see ... teddy bears.

I can see ... balls.

I can see ...

2 What are Nelly's hobbies? Talk to your partner.

Übungsseite

Hobbies

1 What are Sally, Ben and Tina's hobbies? Look and say.

Sally likes skateboarding and ...

Ben likes ... and in-line skating.

Tina likes ... and ...

2 Read the text. Then make your own text.

Hi there.

I'm Kendra from Glasgow.

I'm nine.

I like playing football.

What's your hobby?

The circle of the year

1.41

1.42

1. Listen to the story.

2. What can Lily, Ben and John do in spring?

3. What can Lily, Ben and John do in summer?

4. What can Lily, Ben and John do in autumn?

5. What can Lily, Ben and John do in winter?

6. What flowers can you see?

7. Where is the cat?

* What is Nelly wearing in summer?

Weather and clothes

1.44

1 Listen and point.

2 Put on your ... Take your ... Play with your partner.

- It's sunny.
- It's rainy.
- It's windy.
- It's snowy.
- It's hot.
- It's cold.

Seasons and activities

(1) Look and read. Then talk to your partner.

In spring I like riding my bike.

In summer I like eating ice-cream.

In autumn I like flying my kite.

In winter I like building a snowman.

(2) Read the text. Then make your own text.

Hi. I'm Robert from Liverpool.
My favourite season is spring.
In spring I like in-line skating.
What's your favourite season?

Dialoge führen, Differenzierung

At home

1.47

1. Listen to the story.
2. What can you see in the living room?
3. What toys are in the children's room?
4. Which rooms are upstairs?

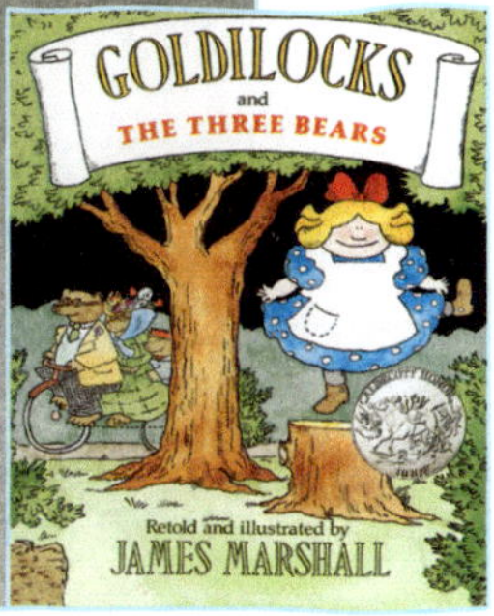

5. Which rooms are downstairs?

6. What is in the wardrobe of the bedroom?

7. Where is the missing sock?

* Where do Squeaky and Nelly look for the sock?

Rooms and furniture

⊙ 1.48

⊙ 14

1 This funny house. Do the chant.

The  is in the living room.

The  is in the children's room.

The  is in the kitchen.

The  is in the bedroom.

The walls are painted yellow.

This funny house is upside down. 

The  is at the door.

The  is on the floor.

The  is on two chairs.

The  is on the stairs.

The telly is on the roof.

I think I'd better move. 

2 Spot the differences. Look and say.

John's room. Picture 1.

John's teddy bear is <u>on</u> the bed.
John's toy car is ... the bed.
John's skipping rope is ... the desk.
John's ball is ...
John's book is ...

John's room. Picture 2.

John's teddy bear is <u>under</u> the bed.
John's toy car is ... the wardrobe.
John's skipping rope is ... the desk.
John's ball is ...
John's book is ...

Where is Squeaky?

1 Which word is missing? Make sentences. Then talk to your partner.

Squeaky is ... the bed.

Squeaky is ... the armchair.

Squeaky is ... the table.

Squeaky is ... the cupboard.

in | on | behind | in | under | on | on | in

Squeaky is ... the wardrobe.

Squeaky is ... the shelf.

Squeaky is ... the bath.

Squeaky is ... the lamp.

2 Listen and check. Point at the pictures.

1.50

3 Read the text. Then make your own text.

Hi, I'm Katie from Chicago.
I live in a house.
Our house has got five rooms.
Where do you live?

At the restaurant

2.02

1. Listen to the story.
2. Who can you see in the picture?
3. How many children can you see?
4. What can you eat at the restaurant?

5. What is the dish of the day?

* What is Nelly having?

6. How much is the hamburger?

Food and drink

1 Look and say.

2.03

16

2 100 cookies. Sing the song.

100 cookies hidden in a tin.
Tommy takes 10.
How many are still in?

90 cookies hidden in a tin.
Tommy takes 10.
How many are still in?

80 cookies hidden in a tin.
Tommy takes 10.
How many are still in?

70 cookies hidden in a tin.
Tommy takes 10.
How many are still in?

60 cookies hidden in a tin.
Tommy takes 10.
How many are still in?

...

10 last cookies hidden in a tin.
Tommy takes 10. Now it's an empty tin.

Food and drink

1 I would like some apple juice. Do the chant.

2.05

17

I would like some apple juice. 

Together with some fish. 

Spaghetti with some chocolate sauce. 

That's my favourite dish. 

2 Act out dialogues.

3 Read the text. Then make your own text.

Good morning.
I'm Ravi from London.
My favourite dish is rice with vegetables.
What's your favourite dish?

At the supermarket

2.12

1. Listen to the story.
2. Which kind of ice-cream can you get here?
3. Which kind of ice-cream would Lily like?
4. Which kind of ice-cream would Ben like?

5. What toys can you get at the supermarket? * How much has Mum to pay?

Ice-cream – ice-cream

2.13 19

1 Ice-cream – ice-cream. Do the chant.

Ice-cream – ice-cream
Which one would you like?
 and 
That's what I like.

Ice-cream – ice-cream
Which one would you like?
 and 
That's what I like.

Ice-cream – ice-cream
Which one would you like?
 and 
That's what I like.

2.14

2 Make your own chant.

3 Which school things can you see? How much is it?

Übungsseite

Let's go and buy ice-cream

1 Listen. Then play with your partner.

2.15

Hello.	Hello.
What would you like?	I'd like some ice-cream, please.
Which one would you like?	Lemon ice-cream, please.
	How much is it?
That's 70 pence.	Here you are.
Thank you. Bye-bye.	Bye-bye.

2 Read the text. Then make your own text.

Hello, I'm Rona from Dublin.
I like vanilla ice-cream best.
What about you?

Dialoge führen, Differenzierung

At the vet

2.20

1. Listen to the story.

2. How many children can you see?

3. How many animals are there at the vet?

4. What is the name of Ben's cat?

5. Where is the fish?

* What about Nelly. Is she ill, too?

Animals

2.21
21

1 Do the chant.

Stretch like a  – jump like a  .

Hop like a  – run like a  .

Swim like a  – sleep like a  .

Kneel like a  – hang like a  .

Climb like a  – play like a  .

Eat like a  – sit on your chair.

2.23

2 Guess the animals. Listen, point and say: It's a ...

Animals

1 Where are the animals? Look and say.

The pig is in the mud. The ... is ... pond.

in	on	under	next to	in front of	behind

2 Read the text. Then make your own text.

Hello.
I'm Simon from New York City.
I have got a dog.
I like my dog very much.
I don't like cats. Do you like cats?

Dialoge führen, Differenzierung

On the move

2.27

1

2

3

4

5

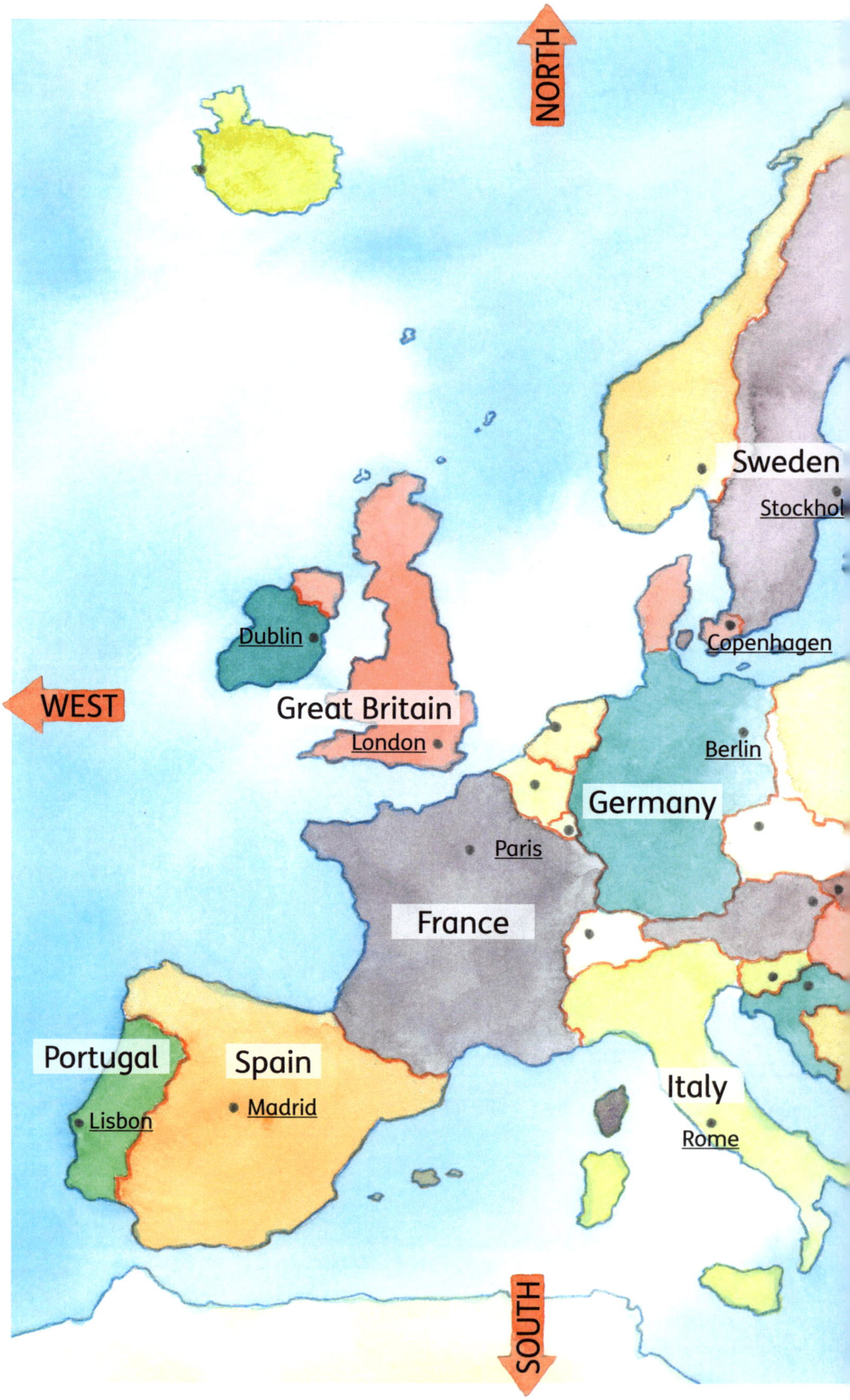

1. Listen to the story.

2. Which number is the British flag?

3. What colours are in the British flag?

4. What is the capital of Great Britain?

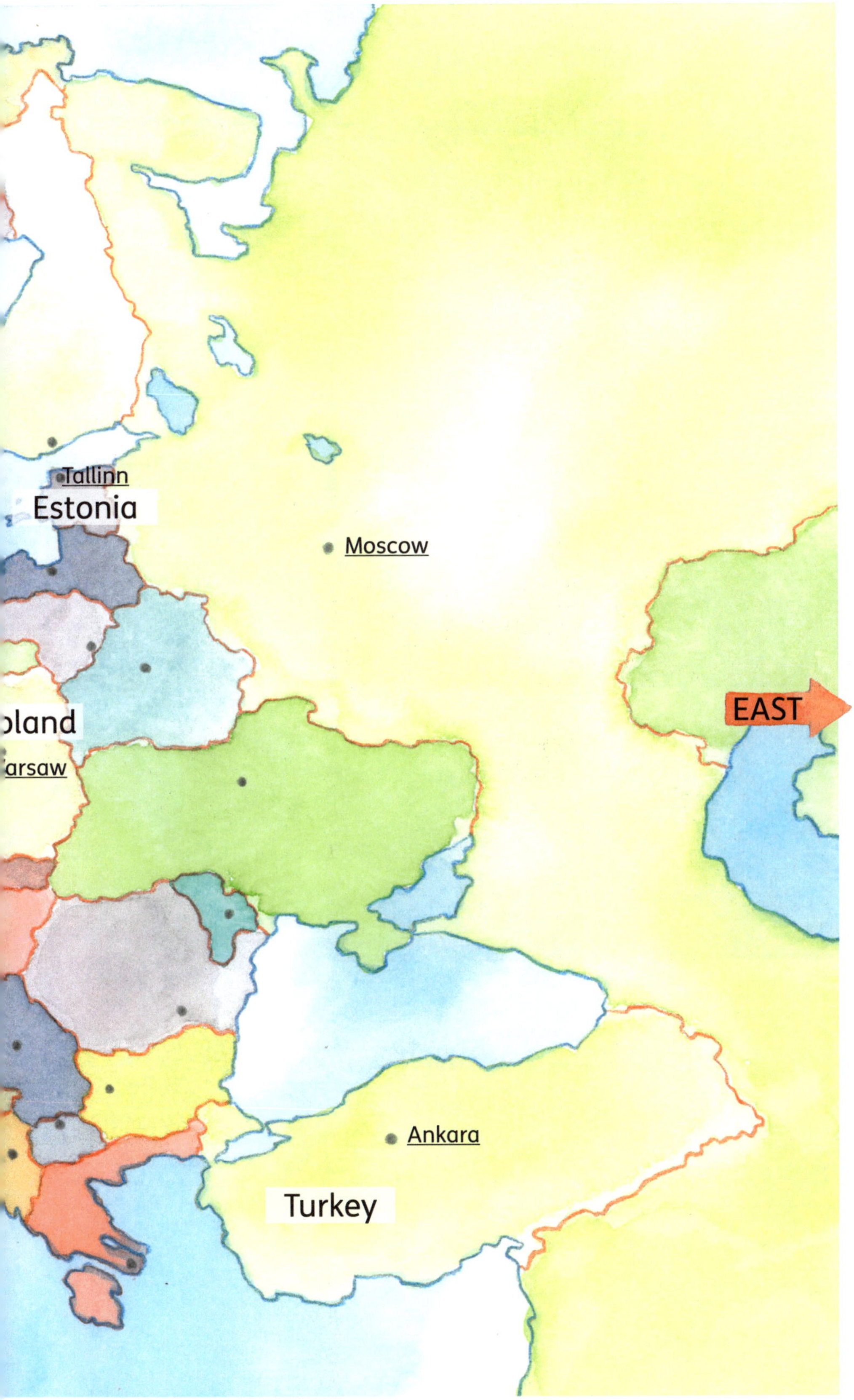

6

7

8

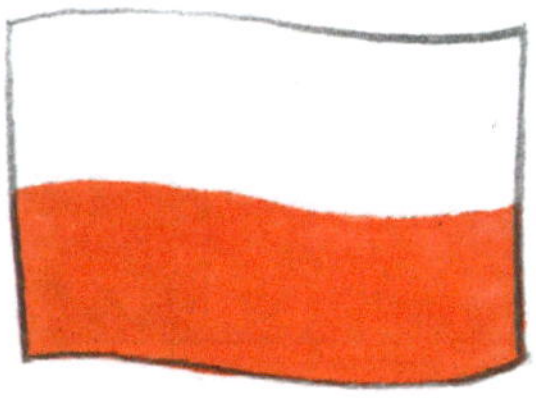

9

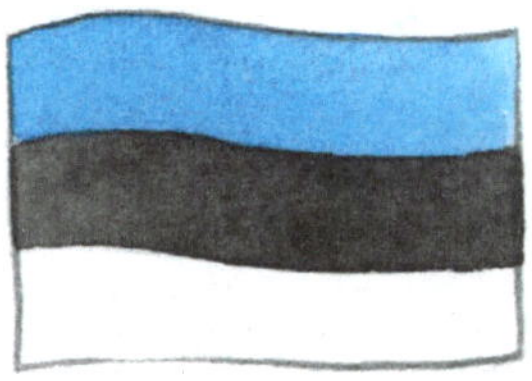

10

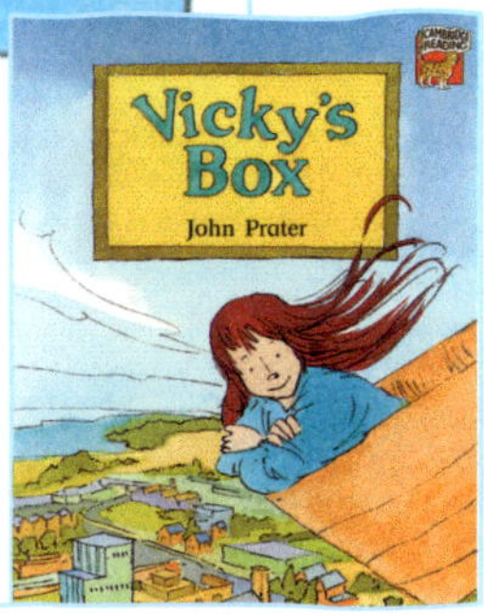

5. Which countries on the map do you know?

* Which number is the German flag?

Let's go to ...

2.28
23

1 Puffertrain. Sing the song.

Puffertrain, puffertrain,
noisy little puffertrain,
if you're going to the sea,
puffertrain, oh please, take me.
Pf-ff-ff, Sh-sh,sh,
noisy little puffertrain.

2.30

2 Different places. Listen and point.

3 Make sentences. Point at the photos and talk to your partner.

Let's go to ...
the sea.
London.
the forest.
the mountains.
the toy museum.
the old castle.
the zoo.
the lake.

Übungsseite

Vehicles

1 Listen and point.

2.31

2 What are they saying? Look and say.

Tom

Tina

Ben

Jenny

Sally

Tom: Let's go by plane.

Tina: Let's go ...

3 Read the text. Then make your own text.

Hi there.

I'm Tina from Great Britain.

I go on holiday by car.

I like holidays in the mountains.

I like hiking. And you?

The story of the three little pigs

2.35

2.36

1) We want to build a little house.

2) Can I have your straw, please?

5) So I'll huff and I'll puff and I'll blow your house down.

6) Can I have your bricks, please?

1. Listen to the story.

2. What are the names of the three little pigs?

3. How many houses do the pigs build altogether?

4. Which house is the best one?

3) Hey, little pig. Open the door and let me in!

4) Can I have your twigs, please?

7) Little pig, here I come!

8) Goodbye, Mr Wolf.

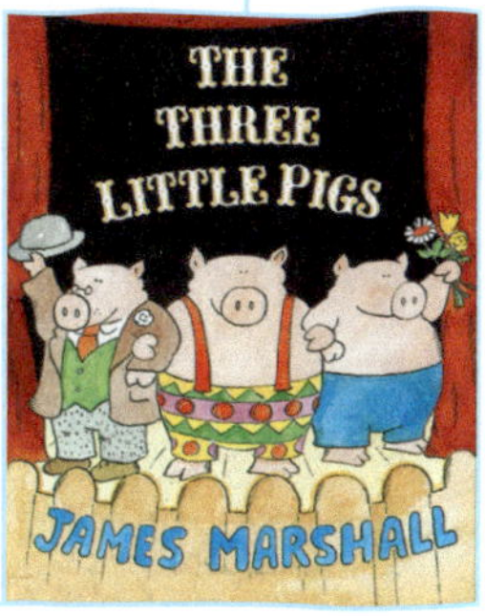

5. Who wants to blow the houses down?
* At the end of the story the pigs sing a song. Can you sing the song?

Let's celebrate! Halloween

2.40

1 Listen and point.

2.41

2 Sing the song.

27

Hey-ho for Halloween.
All the witches can be seen.
Some in black and some in green.
Hey-ho for Halloween.

Landeskunde

1. Listen to the story.
* Where is the hat of the witch?

2.45

2.46

29

1 Listen and point.

2 Sing the song.

We wish you a merry Christmas,
We wish you a merry Christmas,
We wish you a merry Christmas,
And a happy New Year.

Landeskunde

1. Listen to the story.
* What day is it?

Let's celebrate! Pancake Day

2.49 **1** Listen and look at the picture.

Pancake Day is in February.
Mummies bake pancakes and they take part in pancake races.
There are a lot of pancake races in England today.

2.50 **2** Listen to the rhyme.

31 **3** Read the rhyme. Then say the rhyme.

Mix a pancake,
Stir a pancake,
Pop it in a pan,
Fry the pancake,
Toss the pancake,
Catch it, if you can.

Landeskunde

1. Listen to the story.
* In which season is Pancake Day?

1 Sing the song.

2.54
33
2.53

Hot cross buns, hot cross buns!
One a penny, two a penny, hot cross buns!
If you have no daughters, give them to your sons.
One a penny, two a penny, hot cross buns.

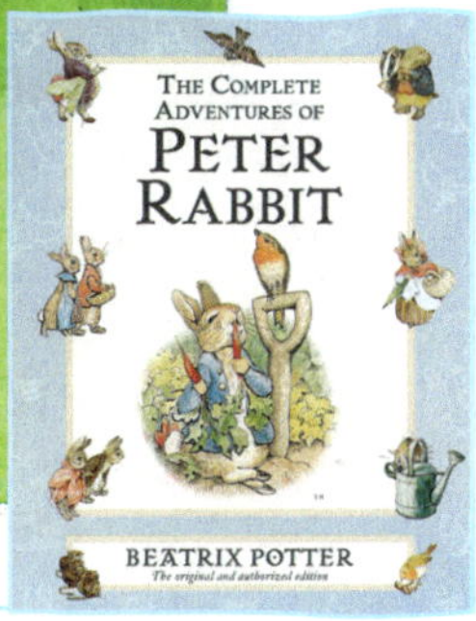

1. Listen to the story.
2. How many Easter eggs can you count?

* What flowers can you see?

Let's celebrate! Happy birthday!

2.58

35

1 Sing the birthday song.

Oh, it's time to sing a song,
to sing a song, to sing a song.
Oh it's time to sing a song,
to sing a birthday song.

Landeskunde

1. Listen to the story.
2. How many children can you see?

* When is your birthday?

1 Sing the summer song.

2.62

36

I like the summer. I like the holidays.
I like the summer. I like to get away.
I like the holidays and to get away.
Dum-di-da-di, dum-di-da-di.
Dum-di-da-di, dum-di-da-di.

1. Listen to the story.
* What is Lily playing?

My words – Classroom phrases

Sit in a circle.

Look at the picture.

Point at the cat.

Show me your pencil case.

Colour in.

Be quiet, please.

Cut out.

Come to the board, please.

Number the pictures.

den Unterrichtsablauf organisieren

My words – Classroom phrases

Give me the pencil, please.

Write down the word.

Open your book.

Listen to the story.

Draw a snowman.

Talk to your partner.

Read the sentences.

Glue the pieces together.

Tick the correct word.

Our exciting Nelly Quiz

1 Use your Pupil's Book and answer the questions.

 Unit 1: What is Nelly playing?  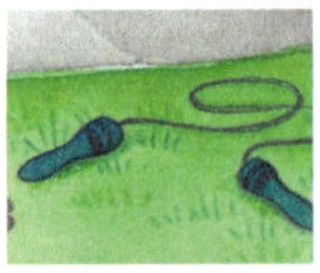

 Unit 2: What colour is Nelly's pencil-case?  

 Unit 3: What is Nelly wearing at the shop?  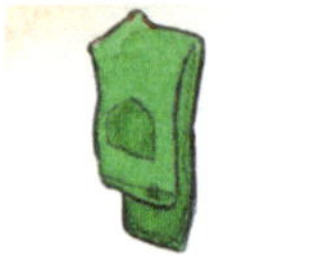

 Unit 4: What has Nelly got in her hands?  

 Unit 5: What is Nelly doing in spring?  

 Unit 6: What are Squeaky and Nelly looking for?  

 Unit 7: What is Nelly having at the restaurant?  

 Unit 8: Which sweets does Nelly like best?  

 Unit 9: Who is sitting next to Nelly?  

 Unit 10: Where does Nelly come from?  

Unit 1: **a ball game**
Unit 2: **orange**
Unit 3: **orange boots**
Unit 4: **a Christmas star**
Unit 5: **picking flowers**
Unit 6: **for the red sock**
Unit 7: **fish and salad**
Unit 8: **jelly beans**
Unit 9: **Sally**
Unit 10: **from Scotland**

Symbolkarten 1 - Beilage 1 zu Pupil's Book 3

Die Symbolkarten eignen sich für die Anbahnung von Redestrukturen.
Die Symbole können bestimmten Fragen zugeordnet werden.

© Ernst Klett Verlag, Stuttgart 2013
© Ernst Klett Verlag, Stuttgart 2013
© Ernst Klett Verlag, Stuttgart 2013
© Ernst Klett Verlag, Stuttgart 2013
© Ernst Klett Verlag, Stuttgart 2013
© Ernst Klett Verlag, Stuttgart 2013
© Ernst Klett Verlag, Stuttgart 2013

Symbolkarten 2 - Beilage 2 zu Pupil's Book 3

Die Symbolkarten eignen sich für die Anbahnung von Redestrukturen.
Die Symbole können bestimmten Fragen zugeordnet werden.

© Ernst Klett Verlag, Stuttgart 2013
© Ernst Klett Verlag, Stuttgart 2013
© Ernst Klett Verlag, Stuttgart 2013
© Ernst Klett Verlag, Stuttgart 2013
© Ernst Klett Verlag, Stuttgart 2013
© Ernst Klett Verlag, Stuttgart 2013
© Ernst Klett Verlag, Stuttgart 2013

Fragekarten 1 - Beilage 3 zu Pupil's Book 3

Zu den blauen Fragekarten gehören die orangefarbenen Antwortkarten. Diese werden in Einzel- oder Partnerabeit zugeordnet. Die Kinder lesen die Fragen und Antworten vor.

What's your name?	How are you?
How old are you?	When is your birthday?
Where do you live?	Where are you from?
What's your favourite ...?	What's your hobby?

Fragekarten 2 - Beilage 4 zu Pupil's Book 3

Zu den blauen Fragekarten gehören die orangefarbenen Antwortkarten. Diese werden in Einzel- oder Partnerarbeit zugeordnet. Die Kinder lesen die Fragen und Antworten vor.

Have you got a ...?	Is it ...?
I like .... And you?	Do you like ...?
What ... do you like best?	How many ... can you see?
What's the weather like today?	What time is it?

© Ernst Klett Verlag, Stuttgart 2013
© Ernst Klett Verlag, Stuttgart 2013
© Ernst Klett Verlag, Stuttgart 2013
© Ernst Klett Verlag, Stuttgart 2013
© Ernst Klett Verlag, Stuttgart 2013
© Ernst Klett Verlag, Stuttgart 2013
© Ernst Klett Verlag, Stuttgart 2013

Antwortkarten 1 - Beilage 5 zu Pupil's Book 3

Die orangefarbenen Antwortkarten werden den blauen Fragekarten in Einzel- oder Partnerabeit zugeordnet. Die Kinder lesen die Fragen und Antworten vor.

My name is	I'm fine, thanks.
I'm ... years old.	My birthday is in ....
I live in ...	I'm from Germany.
My favourite ... is ...	My hobby is ...

© Ernst Klett Verlag, Stuttgart 2013
© Ernst Klett Verlag, Stuttgart 2013
© Ernst Klett Verlag, Stuttgart 2013
© Ernst Klett Verlag, Stuttgart 2013
© Ernst Klett Verlag, Stuttgart 2013
© Ernst Klett Verlag, Stuttgart 2013
© Ernst Klett Verlag, Stuttgart 2013

Antwortkarten 2 - Beilage 6 zu Pupil's Book 3

Die orangefarbenen Antwortkarten werden den blauen Fragekarten in Einzel- oder Partnerabeit zugeordnet. Die Kinder lesen die Fragen und Antworten vor.

Yes, I have got a … No, I haven't got a …	Yes, it is. No, it isn't.
I like …	Yes, I do. No, I don't.
I like … best.	I can see …
Today it's …	It's … o'clock.

© Ernst Klett Verlag, Stuttgart 2013
© Ernst Klett Verlag, Stuttgart 2013
© Ernst Klett Verlag, Stuttgart 2013
© Ernst Klett Verlag, Stuttgart 2013
© Ernst Klett Verlag, Stuttgart 2013
© Ernst Klett Verlag, Stuttgart 2013
© Ernst Klett Verlag, Stuttgart 2013

Domino 1 - Beilage 7 zu Pupil's Book 3

Die Spielkarten werden gemischt und dann unter zwei oder vier Spielern aufgeteilt. Nun legen die Spieler die passenden Karten aneinander und lesen die Fragen und Antworten vor.

	What's your name?	My name is Tom.	How are you?
I'm fine, thanks.	When is your birthday?	My birthday is in June.	How old are you?
Im eight years old.	Where do you live?	I live in Dresden.	Where are you from?
I'm from Germany.	What's your favourite colour?	My favourite colour is blue.	What's your hobby?

© Ernst Klett Verlag, Stuttgart 2013
© Ernst Klett Verlag, Stuttgart 2013
© Ernst Klett Verlag, Stuttgart 2013
© Ernst Klett Verlag, Stuttgart 2013
© Ernst Klett Verlag, Stuttgart 2013
© Ernst Klett Verlag, Stuttgart 2013
© Ernst Klett Verlag, Stuttgart 2013

Domino 2 - Beilage 8 zu Pupil's Book 3

Die Spielkarten werden gemischt und dann unter zwei oder vier Spielern aufgeteilt. Nun legen die Spieler die passenden Karten aneinander und lesen die Fragen und Antworten vor.

My hobby is playing football.	Do you like swimming?	Yes, I do.	What's your favourite toy?
My favourite toy is my toy car.	Have you got a brother or a sister?	I have got a sister.	What's your favourite food?
My favourite food is pizza.	What's your favourite drink?	My favourite drink is apple juice.	Have you got a pet?
Yes, I have got a cat.	What's the weather like today?	Today it's sunny.	

© Ernst Klett Verlag, Stuttgart 2013
© Ernst Klett Verlag, Stuttgart 2013
© Ernst Klett Verlag, Stuttgart 2013
© Ernst Klett Verlag, Stuttgart 2013
© Ernst Klett Verlag, Stuttgart 2013
© Ernst Klett Verlag, Stuttgart 2013
© Ernst Klett Verlag, Stuttgart 2013